MY FIRST
SPANISH
PHRASES

Thank you.
Gracias.
(GRAH-see-ahs)

What is your name?
¿Cómo te llamas?
(KOH-moh tay YAH-mahs)

BY
JILL KALZ

ILLUSTRATED BY
DANIELE FABBRI

TRANSLATOR
TRANSLATIONS.COM

PICTURE WINDOW BOOKS
a capstone imprint

TABLE OF CONTENTS

HOW TO USE THIS DICTIONARY

This book is full of useful phrases in both English and Spanish. The English phrase appears first, followed by the Spanish phrase. Look below each Spanish phrase for help to sound it out. Try reading the phrases aloud.

Topic heading in English

Topic heading in Spanish

Additional phrases to learn

Phrase in English
Phrase in Spanish
(pronunciation)

NOTES ABOUT THE SPANISH LANGUAGE

Nouns in Spanish are masculine or feminine. For example, the word "teacher" would be "maestro" for a male teacher. The word changes to "maestra" if the teacher is female.

The forms of many adjectives change to match the noun. The change is slight. In most cases, the ending of an adjective changes from an "o" (masculine) to an "a" (feminine) ending.

For example, in the phrase "I feel scared," the word "scared" is written as "asustado" if the speaker is male. The word changes to "asustada" if the speaker is female.

In this phrase book, the phrases match the gender of the characters shown on each page.

LETTERS OF THE ALPHABET
AND THEIR PRONUNCIATIONS

A a • ah

B b • beh

C c • seh

D d • deh

E e • eh

F f • EH-feh

G g • heh

H h • AH-che

I i • ee

J j • HOH-tah

K k • kah

L l • EH-leh

M m • EH-meh

N n • EH-neh

Ñ ñ • EH-nyeh

O o • oh

P p • peh

Q q • koo

R r • EH-rreh

S s • EH-seh

T t • teh

U u • oo

V v • beh

W w • DOH-bleh beh

X x • AY-kees

Y y • ee gree-AY-gah

Z z • SEH-tah

IT SOUNDS *LIKE*

There are 27 letters in the Spanish alphabet. These letters include the 26 letters of the English alphabet, plus the letter "ñ." Most of these letters sound the same. But there are some letters in Spanish that sound different. You can use this guide to learn how to say these sounds in Spanish.

	SOUND	PRONUNCIATION	EXAMPLES
CONSONANTS	c (ca, co, cu)	like c in coat	caracol kah-rah-KOHL
	c (ce, ci)	like s in send	cine SEE-nay
	ch	like ch in chin	noche NOH-chay
	g (ga, go, gu)	like g in go	golpe GOHL-pay
	g (ge, gi)	like h in house	genio HAY-nee-oh
	gue, gui	like g in gate	juguete hoo-GAY-tay
	h	silent, like h in hour	hambre AHM-bray
	j	like h in house but stronger	jirafa hee-RAH-pha
	ll	like y in yet	cepillo say-PEE-yoh
	ñ	like ny in canyon	baño BAH-nyoh
	rr	sounds like a very strong r	perro PAYR-roh
	que, qui	like k in ketchup	parque PAHR-kay

	SOUND	PRONUNCIATION	EXAMPLES
VOWELS	a	like a in hat	gato GAH-toh
	e	like ay in hay	leche LAY-chay
	i	like ee in bee	cocina koh-SEE-nah
	o	like o in note	tractor TRAHK-tohr
	u	like oo in food	azul ah-SOOL

	SOUND	PRONUNCIATION	EXAMPLES
VOWEL COMBINATIONS	ei/ey	like ey in grey	rey RAY-ee
	oi/oy	like oy in boy	estoy ehs-TOY
	au	like ou in sound	aula AH-oo-lah

Spanish: LO BÁSICO (loh BAH-see-koh)

Thank you.
Gracias.
(GRAH-see-ahs)

You are welcome.
De nada.
(day NAH-dah)

What is your name?
¿Cómo te llamas?
(KOH-moh tay YAH-mahs)

My name is___.
Me llamo___.
(may YAH-moh___)

MORE TO LEARN

Yes	No
Sí	**No**
(see)	(noh)

I live in an apartment.
Vivo en un apartamento.
(VEE-voh ehn oon ah-pahr-tah-MAYN-toh)

Where do you live?
¿Dónde vives?
(DOHN-deh VEE-vas)

a house
una casa
(OO-nah KAH-sah)

My address is _____.
Mi dirección es ___.
(mee dee-rehk-see-OHN ehs ____)

MORE TO LEARN

My phone number is _____.
Mi teléfono es _____.
(mee teh-LAY-foh-noh ehs___)
See page 30 for numbers.

Are you hungry?
¿Tienes hambre?
(tee-AY-nehs AHM-bray)

I am hungry.
Tengo hambre.
(TAYN-goh AHM-bray)

thirsty
sed
(said)

What is for supper?
¿Qué hay de comida?
(kay eye day koh-MEE-dah)

lunch
almuerzo
(ahl-MWER-soh)

breakfast
desayuno
(day-sah-YOO-noh)

MORE TO LEARN

I am not hungry.
No tengo hambre.
(noh TAYN-goh AHM-bray)

English: **FAMILY**

This is my mother.
Esta es mi mamá.
(EHS-tah ehs mee mah-MAH)

This is my aunt and uncle.
Estos son mi tía y mi tío.
(EHS-tohs sohn mee TEE-ah ee mee TEE-oh)

my grandma and grandpa
mi abuela y mi abuelo
(mee ah-BWAY-lah ee mee ah-BWAY-loh)

Her/His name is ___.
Se llama ___.
(say YAH-mah ___)

Spanish: LA FAMILIA (lah fah-MEE-lee-ah)

Do you speak English?
¿Hablas inglés?
(AH-blahs een-GLAYS)

Spanish
español
(ehs-pah-NYOHL)

German
alemán
(ah-lay-MAHN)

French
francés
(frahn-SAYS)

Chinese
chino
(CHEE-noh)

A little.
Un poco.
(oon POH-koh)

DUTY FREE

7 8 9 10 11 12

MORE TO LEARN

father
papá
(pah-PAH)

sister
hermana
(air-MAH-nah)

brother
hermano
(air-MAH-noh)

15

Spanish: LA FECHA Y LA HORA (lah FAY-chah ee lah OR-ah)

Today is Saturday.
Hoy es sábado.
(oy ehs SAH-bah-doh)

Tomorrow is Sunday.
Mañana es domingo.
(mah-NYAH-nah ehs doh-MEEN-goh)

Yesterday was Friday.
Ayer fue viernes.
(ah-YEHR fway vee-AYR-nehs)

MORE TO LEARN

Sunday
domingo
(doh-MEEN-goh)

Monday
lunes
(LOO-nehs)

Tuesday
martes
(MAHR-tays)

Wednesday
miércoles
(mee-AYR-koh-lehs)

Thursday
jueves
(HWAY-vays)

Friday
viernes
(vee-AYR-nehs)

Saturday
sábado
(SAH-bah-doh)

Spanish: LOS MESES Y LAS ESTACIONES

(lohs MEH-says ee lahs ehs-tah-see-OHN-ays)

I love <u>summer</u>!
¡Me encanta el verano!
(may ehn-KAHN-tah ehl veh-RAH-noh)

fall
el otoño
(ehl oh-TOH-nyoh)

winter
el invierno
(ehl een-vee-EHR-noh)

spring
la primavera
(lah pree-mah-VEH-rah)

MORE TO LEARN

January
enero
(eh-NAY-roh)

February
febrero
(feh-BRAY-roh)

March
marzo
(MAHR-soh)

April
abril
(ah-BREEL)

May
mayo
(MAH-yoh)

June
junio
(HOO-nee-oh)

July
julio
(HOO-lee-oh)

August
agosto
(ah-GOHS-toh)

September
septiembre
(sehp-tee-EHM-breh)

October
octubre
(ohk-TOO-breh)

November
noviembre
(noh-vee-EHM-breh)

December
diciembre
(dee-see-EHM-breh)

It is cold.
Hace frío.
(AH-say FREE-oh)

hot
calor
(kah-LOHR)

sunny
sol
(sohl)

Wear a coat.
Ponte un abrigo.
(POHN-tay oon ah-BREE-goh)

boots
las botas
(lahs BOH-tahs)

hat
un sombrero
(oon sohm-BRAY-roh)

mittens
los guantes
(lohs goo-AHN-tays)

We study science.
Estudiamos ciencias.
(ehs-too-dee-AH-mohs see-EHN-see-ahs)

math
matemáticas
(mah-tay-MAH-tee-kahs)

history
historia
(ees-TOH-ree-ah)

May I use your pencil?
¿Puedo usar tu lápiz?
(poo-EH-doh oo-SAHR too LAH-pees)

scissors
las tijeras
(lahs tee-HAY-rahs)

glue
el pegamento
(ehl pay-gah-MEHN-toh)

MORE TO LEARN

My teacher is___.
Mi maestra es___.
(mee mah-ES-trah ehs___)

This is my favorite book!
¡Este es mi libro favorito!
(EHS-tay ehs mee LEE-broh fah-voh-REE-toh)

Where is the bathroom?
¿Dónde está el baño?
(DOHN-day ehs-TAH ehl BAH-nyoh)

lunchroom
el comedor
(ehl koh-may-DOHR)

bus stop
la parada del autobús
(lah pah-RAH-dah dayl ahw-toh-BOOS)

Are you ready for the test?
¿Estás lista para la prueba?
(ehs-TAHS LEES-tah PAH-rah lah proo-AY-bah)

Go right.
Ve a la derecha.
(vay ah lah day-RAY-chah)

Go straight ahead.
Sigue derecho.
(SEE-gay day-RAY-choh)

Go left.
Ve a la izquierda.
(vay ah lah ees-kee-AYR-dah)

I forgot.
Se me olvidó.
(say may ohl-vee-DOH)

___ is my friend.
___ es mi amigo.
(___ ehs mee ah-MEE-goh)

What's up?
¿Qué pasa?
(kay PAH-sah)

That's cool!
¡Es estupendo!
(ehs ehs-too-PAYN-doh)

MORE TO LEARN

No way!
¡Ni hablar!
(nee ah-BLAR)

Lame!
¡Flojo!
(FLOH-hoh)

Numbers • LOS NÚMEROS (lohs NOO-may-rohs)

1 one • **uno** (OO-noh)

2 two • **dos** (dohs)

3 three • **tres** (trays)

4 four • **cuatro** (KWAH-troh)

5 five • **cinco** (SEEN-koh)

6 six • **seis** (SAY-ees)

7 seven • **siete** (see-EH-tay)

8 eight • **ocho** (OH-choh)

9 nine • **nueve** (noo-AY-vay)

10 ten • **diez** (dee-EHS)

11 eleven • **once** (OWN-say)

12 twelve • **doce** (DOH-say)

13 thirteen • **trece** (TRAY-say)

14 fourteen • **catorce** (ka-TOR-say)

15 fifteen • **quince** (KEEN-say)

16 sixteen • **dieciséis** (de-ay-see-SAY-ees)

17 seventeen • **diecisiete** (de-ay-see-see-EH-tay)

18 eighteen • **dieciocho** (de-ay-see-OH-choh)

19 nineteen • **diecinueve** (de-ay-see-noo-AY-vay)

20 twenty • **veinte** (BAYN-tay)

30 thirty • **treinta** (TRAYN-tah)

40 forty • **cuarenta** (kwa-RAYN-tah)

50 fifty • **cincuenta** (seen-KWAYN-tah)

60 sixty • **sesenta** (say-SAYN-tah)

70 seventy • **setenta** (say-TAYN-tah)

80 eighty • **ochenta** (oh-CHAYN-tah)

90 ninety • **noventa** (noh-VAYN-tah)

100 one hundred • **cien** (see-AYN)

Colors · LOS COLORES (lohs koh-LOHR-ehs)

 red • **rojo**
(ROH-hoh)

 purple • **violeta**
(vee-oh-LAY-tah)

 orange • **anaranjado**
(ah-nah-rahn-HAH-doh)

 pink • **rosado**
(roh-SAH-doh)

 yellow • **amarillo**
(ah-mah-REE-yoh)

 brown • **marrón**
(mar-RONE)

 green • **verde**
(VAIR-day)

 black • **negro**
(NAY-groh)

 blue • **azul**
(ah-SOOL)

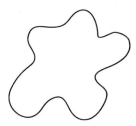 white • **blanco**
(BLAHN-koh)

READ MORE

Kudela, Katy R. *My First Book of Spanish Words.* Bilingual Picture Dictionaries. Mankato, Minn.: Capstone Press, 2010.

Modéré, Armelle. *My First Spanish-English Dictionary of Sentences.* Hauppauge, N.Y.: Barron's, 2007.

Stanley, Mandy. *My First Spanish Book.* Boston: Kingfisher, 2007.

INTERNET SITES

FactHound offers a safe, fun way to find Internet sites related to this book. All of the sites on FactHound have been researched by our staff.

Here's all you do:

Visit *www.facthound.com*

Type in this code: 9781404871526

Check out projects, games and lots more at **www.capstonekids.com**

LOOK FOR ALL THE BOOKS IN THE SPEAK ANOTHER LANGUAGE! SERIES:

MY FIRST FRENCH *PHRASES*

MY FIRST GERMAN *PHRASES*

MY FIRST MANDARIN CHINESE *PHRASES*

MY FIRST SPANISH *PHRASES*

Editor: Katy Kudela
Designer: Alison Thiele
Art Director: Nathan Gassman
Production Specialist: Danielle Ceminsky
The illustrations in this book were created digitally.

Picture Window Books
1710 Roe Crest Drive
North Mankato, Minnesota 56003
www.capstonepub.com

 All books published by Picture Window Books are manufactured with paper containing at least 10 percent post-consumer waste.

Library of Congress Cataloging-in-Publication Data
Kalz, Jill.
  My first Spanish phrases / by Jill Kalz; illustrated by
    Daniele Fabbri.
      p. cm.—(Nonfiction picture books : Speak
  another language)
  Includes bibliographical references and index.
  Summary: "Simple text paired with themed illustrations invite the reader to learn to speak Spanish"—Provided by publisher.
  ISBN 978-1-4048-7152-6 (library binding)
  ISBN 978-1-4048-7247-9 (paperback)
    1. Spanish language—Textbooks for foreign speakers—English—Juvenile literature. 2. Spanish language—Conversation and phrase books—English—Juvenile literature.
  I. Title.
  PC4129.E5K25 2012
    468.3'421—dc23   2011027189

Printed in the United States of America in North Mankato, Minnesota.
042013   007267R